CW01512624

Original title:
Quiet Dabs Over the Phoenix Murk

Author: Liina Liblikas
ISBN HARDBACK: 978-1-80562-635-0
ISBN PAPERBACK: 978-1-80564-156-8

Through the Haze of Forgotten Voices

In shadows deep, the whispers dwell,
Forgotten tales, enchanted spell.
Each echo sings of days gone by,
In every heart, a wish to fly.

Beneath the stars, where dreams converge,
A tapestry of souls emerge.
They speak in hushed, elusive tones,
Their stories linger, like old stones.

Through misty paths, their laughter fades,
Adrift in time, where magic wades.
The voices call, a siren's plea,
In memory's grip, we dare to see.

A dance of ghosts, in moonlit grace,
They weave through dreams, a soft embrace.
With every heartbeat, time stands still,
In the forgotten, we find our thrill.

Yet as we tread on this fine line,
We glimpse the past, its gaze divine.
Through hazy veils, we seek to find,
The echoes of a world entwined.

The Inward Journey Amidst Searing Echoes

Inward we wander, through the night,
While shadows twist, and fears take flight.
The echoes of our pain resound,
Yet strength lies deep within the ground.

Each step we take reveals the truth,
A path untouched by fleeting youth.
The silence breaks with every thought,
In searing flames, our battles fought.

Yet from the ash, a phoenix rise,
With wings of courage, it defies.
The journey's hard, the road unclear,
But in the trial, we find our cheer.

Through whispered dreams, we seek the light,
That flickers gently in the night.
With every echo of despair,
We stitch our hearts with tender care.

So onward still, we shall persist,
Through searing echoes, we exist.
The inward journey, brave and bold,
Reveals the truths we long to hold.

Whispers beneath the Ashen Sky

In shadows deep, where silence sighs,
The whispers dance, beneath the skies.
Each secret borne on winds so slight,
Brings tales of woe and flickers of light.

Through ashen clouds, the spirits weave,
Forgotten dreams that still believe.
A flicker here, a shimmer there,
Hope lingers still, beyond despair.

From distant realms, a soft refrain,
Calls out to hearts that know the pain.
With every dusk, a chance to mend,
In twilight's cloak, we find a friend.

Yet here we stand, under the gray,
With every breath, we'll find our way.
So let the whispers guide our flight,
To brighter shores, from darkest night.

Echoes of Hope in Shadowed Flames

In shadows deep, where embers glow,
A fire's warmth begins to grow.
Echoes of hope rise with the smoke,
In every flicker, a promise spoke.

The night is long, but dreams endure,
Each flickering flame, a heart so pure.
Through flickers faint, we seek the dawn,
With every breath, our fears are gone.

From ashes cold, a spark may leap,
Through darkness vast, our spirits creep.
The warmth it brings, we'll nurture slow,
As shadows dance, our courage flows.

In every heart, a beacon bright,
That shines beyond the endless night.
So gather near, and feel the heat,
In shadowed flames, our lives repeat.

Murmurs of Resilience Amidst the Smolder

Beneath the smolder, whispers lie,
Of strength reborn, as ashes cry.
Through bitter trials, we'll take our stand,
With every whisper, we make our plan.

For in the ruins, seeds of change,
We find new paths that feel so strange.
Though fire once raged, now it's still,
Yet hope ignites, with iron will.

The earth may tremble, but roots run deep,
In silent strength, the universe keeps.
With every murmur, we rise anew,
In the heart's embrace, we'll break through.

So let the smoke clear from our eyes,
We bear the weight of ancient ties.
In resilience found, we will create,
A world reborn, where dreams await.

Traces of Light in the Hazy Dawn

When morning breaks with hues so rare,
The traces of light fill the air.
In hazy dawn, the shadows flee,
A canvas washed, once dark, now free.

Each ray a whisper, soft and sweet,
An invitation to rise, to greet.
The world awakes from slumber deep,
In light's embrace, our spirits leap.

With every breath, a chance to see,
The beauty held in mystery.
Through veils of mist, our dreams take flight,
Chasing the echoes of fading night.

In morning's glow, we find our song,
Together, brave, where we belong.
With open hearts, we'll walk the way,
Through traces of light, a brand new day.

Serene Shadows on the Edge of Flame

In twilight's grasp, the shadows dance,
They twirl and weave in silent trance.
A spark ignites, a fleeting sigh,
As embers glow, and old dreams fly.

The whispers of the firelight sing,
Of tales forgotten, of fleeting spring.
With every flicker, a story tells,
Of magic brewing in hidden wells.

In corners dark where secrets hide,
The warmth of flames meets quiet pride.
In shadows deep, the heart finds home,
Among the flickers, it starts to roam.

With every crackle, a moment lost,
While time unfolds, it pays the cost.
Yet, still it shines, this ember's glow,
A dance of life, a gentle flow.

So linger here, beneath the stars,
In tranquil night, embrace your scars.
For every shadow, every flame,
A story written, no two the same.

The Unheard Lullaby of the Phoenix's Rest

In a cradle woven from stardust bright,
The phoenix sleeps through the long, deep night.
With wings unfurled, in silence, she dreams,
Of ancient fires and whispering streams.

Beneath the moon's soft, silvery glow,
A lullaby sings from realms below.
It carries tales of ashes and flame,
Of rebirth and loss, yet never the same.

In slumber's grasp, she dances alone,
Her spirit lifts like a precious stone.
Transcending worlds with every sigh,
In the heart of night, her soul will fly.

With every breath, a promise is made,
For in her rest, a legacy laid.
The unheard music of her rebirth,
Echoes softly across the earth.

Awake, dear one, when the dawn arrives,
And let your heart ignite and thrive.
For in the ashes, your strength will rise,
A phoenix reborn under boundless skies.

Radiance Found in the Whispering Ash

In the remnants of fire, a glimmer ignites,
A spark in the ashes, where darkness invites.
With whispers of hope woven through air,
A past left behind, a reminder, a prayer.

The dance of the embers softly entwined,
A tapestry woven, a treasure defined.
In quiet repose, the world finds her grace,
As flickers of light find their rightful place.

In the cool of the night, a vision appears,
A flame of the heart casting away fears.
For in every shadow, a riddle resides,
A promise of warmth where true magic abides.

In the swirling winds, the stories renew,
Of dreams that were chased and hearts that broke through.

The whispers of ash tell tales of the brave,
Who danced with the fire and learned how to save.

So gaze into embers, let your spirit roam,
In the depths of the quiet, you'll find your way home.
For radiance blooms in the darkest of night,
A beacon that guides us, both gentle and bright.

In the Midst of a Soft Firequake

In gentle tremors, the ground shifts below,
As magic awakens, its currents flow.
Soft flames are rising, with whispers they speak,
Of wonders unseen, and treasures unique.

In the heart of the quaking, a rhythm beats strong,
A dance of the shadows, a haunting song.
With every spark, the night softly quakes,
As dreams take flight in the warmth that awakes.

The world holds its breath, in awe of the night,
As embers swirl 'neath the softest light.
In the midst of the chaos, a calmness prevails,
With fire in bloom, as the nightingale wails.

So linger within this magnetic embrace,
Where fire and heartbeats entwine in their space.
For even amidst turmoil and tear,
The whispers of flames guide us near.

Let the quake remind you of strength in your core,
Of battles you've fought, of the dreams you restore.
In the warmth of the night, find a place to ignite,
For each ember's glow is a magical sight.

Shadows in the Resilient Mist

In the depths where whispers weave,
Shadows dance, though souls believe.
Veils of grey, a haunting tune,
Fleeting glimpses, night's cocoon.

Through the fog, a lantern glows,
Guiding hearts where courage grows.
Ethereal dreams drift and sway,
In the mist, lost spirits play.

Echoes linger, softly call,
In the shadows, no fear at all.
Strength is forged in twilight's blend,
In resilient mists, we mend.

Gently flowing streams of fate,
Amidst the dark, we contemplate.
Life's rich tapestry unfurls,
Through the mist, the magic swirls.

Beneath the boughs where secrets hide,
Hope emerges, our faithful guide.
In each shadow, wisdom kissed,
In the mist, we shall persist.

A Hush Amongst the Phoenix Flames

In the heart where embers soar,
A quiet peace, an ancient lore.
Phoenix whispers, flames that grace,
Carving stories in time and space.

Through the fire, a hush descends,
Life and death, where sorrow mends.
Burnt away, the past takes flight,
Phoenix hearts find brand new light.

Wings unfurl in fiery glow,
From the ashes, dreams shall grow.
Courage spun in threads of fate,
Amongst the flames, we elevate.

In this hush, the world stands still,
Echoes dance, and shadows thrill.
Rise and burn, the cycle reigns,
In the hush, love still remains.

Amidst the blaze, a soft refrain,
From the flames, we break the chain.
A rebirth in the glowing night,
In fiery hues, we find our light.

Tranquil Moments in the Charred Realm

In the ashes, quiet sighs,
Repose blooms beneath the skies.
Charred remains of dreams once bright,
In the stillness, we find light.

Softened whispers, twilight song,
In the realms where shadows throng.
Tranquil hearts begin to mend,
In the charred, we shall transcend.

Echoed dreams like pages turned,
Lessons learned through bridges burned.
Amidst the gray, hope's embers start,
Each charred piece reclaims a heart.

Beneath the wreck, new roots will grow,
In the silence, truths will flow.
Moments here, forever stay,
In this realm, we find our way.

As the night succumbs to dawn,
Charred remains are never gone.
In tranquil moments, we find grace,
In the wreckage, life's embrace.

Fleeting Silence on a Fiery Canvas

On a canvas of red and gold,
Fleeting silence, stories told.
Brushstrokes bright, with flames entwined,
In the quiet, solace find.

Silence dances, shadows play,
In this fire, hearts sway.
Colors bleed and visions bloom,
In this silence, we dispel gloom.

Whispers linger, paints collide,
In the blaze, we cannot hide.
A fleeting moment, vivid dream,
Upon this canvas, thoughts redeem.

Softly burning, passionate sparks,
Light ignites and leaves its marks.
Fleeting shadows, tales take flight,
On fiery canvas, pure delight.

Embers fade but still remain,
In the silence, there's no pain.
Art of fire, heart's embrace,
In fleeting silence, we find grace.

Flickering Hopes in a Smoky Veil

In shadows cast by fading light,
Whispers dance through the night air.
Each flicker speaks of dreams held tight,
While shadows weave tales of despair.

Among the embers, soft and warm,
Hopes flicker, a fragile flame.
In smoky veils, they swirl and swarm,
Binding hearts with whispered names.

The moon peeks through the heavy shroud,
Guiding souls through the thick haze.
Among the lost, a silent crowd,
With flickering dreams in a daze.

A spark ignites the stillness deep,
As secrets rise with each breath.
In the silence, we weep and keep,
The echoes of life mingled with death.

But when the dawn breaks through the dark,
The smoke will clear, the light will play.
In each heart lies a hidden spark,
Flickering hopes on a new day.

A Veil of Ashes and Forgotten Whispers

In the hush where shadows merge,
Ashes fall like silent tears.
Forgotten whispers start to surge,
Haunting echoes of old fears.

Between the ruins, dreams decay,
Lurking in the dust and grime.
The past, a ghost that will not stray,
Tempering hope with whispered rhyme.

Veils of sorrow drape the land,
While whispers dance on worn-out lips.
Through the silence, a guiding hand,
Holds stories of forgotten trips.

Yet in the dark, a spark does bloom,
Pushing past the veil of dread.
From the ashes, a sweet perfume,
Reminds us of the paths we tread.

So gather these whispers, let them soar,
Through the veil of ashes, they wend.
For in each heart lies the lore,
Of hope that whispers, never ends.

Ethereal Calm in a World Ablaze

In a realm where flames take flight,
An ethereal calm descends.
While the world ignites with fierce light,
A stillness in chaos bends.

Through raging fire, soft winds blow,
Caressing the flames in their rage.
In each moment, a hidden glow,
Holds the silence at center stage.

Hearts united, though worlds may burn,
In stillness, the true strength resides.
Through the fire, our spirits learn,
To rise above the raging tides.

With every spark, new beginnings wait,
In the ashes, rebirth will soar.
Calm amidst the tempest's hate,
The embers ignite dreams once more.

So let the blaze light up the night,
In its fury, find the grace.
For each end births another flight,
In the calm, we find our place.

Glimmers of Light in the Mournful Ash

In the depth of the mournful ash,
Glimmers dance like distant stars.
Between the ruins, hopes clash,
Worn down by life's unforgiving bars.

A breath of wind stirs the ground,
Carrying whispers from afar.
In silence, new strength is found,
As dreams awaken, sparked by a scar.

Among the shadows, joy threads through,
Eclipsing the darkness with light.
Each glimmer, a beacon so true,
Guiding lost souls through the night.

The past may loom, a heavy shroud,
But glimmers persist with soft might.
Amidst the chaos, strong and proud,
They promise a path to the bright.

So when the day seems bleak and worn,
Look closely, where glimmers may hide.
For in the ash, a hope reborn,
Lights the way, where dreams abide.

Murmurs in the Depths of Desolation

In shadows deep where silence reigns,
Whispers echo through shattered chains.
Ghostly figures, dreams untold,
Linger softly, growing bold.

Beneath the weight of heavy skies,
Hope flickers dim, a soft disguise.
Roots entwined in sorrow's vines,
Lost in time where despair twines.

Yet through the fog, a glimmer shines,
Breaking through the cursed confines.
A distant call, a spark of light,
Inviting souls to rise from night.

Time weaves tales of lovers lost,
Echoes soft, at what cost?
In the depths, a heartbeat's song,
Faint but steady, sweet and strong.

So linger not in bitter gloom,
For dawn will chase away the doom.
In every murmur, every sigh,
A chance to dream, to soar, to fly.

Lament of the Rising Star

Beneath the veil of twilight's grace,
A starlet weeps in boundless space.
With every tear, a wish takes flight,
To pierce the darkness, claim the light.

Once bright and bold, now dimmed by fears,
Silenced dreams drift on the years.
Yet in her heart, embers glow,
A quiet strength she cannot forgo.

With midnight's breath, she weaves her fate,
Chasing shadows, seeking fate.
In the silence, she finds her way,
A symphony of night and day.

Though tumult threatens to consume,
She rises high beyond the gloom.
A phoenix born from stardust's core,
In every heartbeat, she is more.

So let her soar, let her sing,
For every night gifts dawn's bright ring.
In the echoes of the cosmic sea,
The rising star dares to be free.

Secrets Beneath the Ashen Surface

Amidst the ruins, ashes lie,
Whispers of lives, long gone, sigh.
Each crumbling stone, a tale to tell,
Of laughter, folly, love's sweet spell.

Beneath the layer of charred despair,
Lies a memory, tender and rare.
Fragments glisten in twilight's glow,
Hints of beauty, long laid low.

In the silence, secrets stir,
Glimmers of hope begin to blur.
Through the dark, a heart still beats,
Yearning for life in quiet retreats.

With every breath, the past hails back,
Fires of joy, embers of lack.
Yet from the ash, new dreams arise,
A promise carved in endless skies.

So sift through the remnants, heed the call,
For from the ruins, we rise, we fall.
In the echoes of memories past,
Lies a future bright, meant to last.

Soft Breaths Over the Smoldering Ruins

In the stillness where embers glow,
Breath of the earth speaks soft, though low.
Tales of laughter, joys once shared,
Now linger faintly, hearts laid bare.

Over the stones where shadows creep,
Whispers linger, secrets deep.
Ghostly dances in the night,
Shimmer like stars, fading from sight.

Yet through the haze, a flicker stirs,
The pulse of life in breath-like murmurs.
From disarray, a new path will rise,
Awakening dreams beneath dark skies.

Soot-covered memories paint the ground,
In woven tales, lost voices found.
Soft breaths gather, woven tight,
In the night's embrace, they take flight.

So listen closely, hear their song,
For in the chaos, they belong.
From smoldering ruins, hope ignites,
Softly rising, to claim the nights.

The Tender Bloom After the Blaze

In the ash where shadows dwell,
A gentle seed starts to swell.
Bright petals dance on charred remains,
Hope reborn in golden veins.

Soft whispers float on morning air,
Awakening dreams, tender and rare.
Each dewdrop sings a quiet tune,
Painting worlds beneath the moon.

The sun spills warmth on blackened ground,
In blushing light, new life is found.
It stretches wide with vibrant grace,
A tender bloom in time and space.

Yet memories linger, shadows play,
In the heart where embers sway.
The journey forged in fiery strife,
Turns ash and flame to vibrant life.

So rise, dear bud, embrace the day,
Transform your fears, let them stray.
For in the blaze, a vision grows,
A tender bloom after the throes.

Veils of Stillness in the Wake of Heat

A silence wraps the brittle air,
As heat draws back its fiery stare.
In stillness found where shadows creep,
A tranquil hush invites the deep.

The sun concedes to twilight's grace,
While embers flicker, soft embrace.
The world, aglow with whispered sighs,
As night descends, the solace lies.

Beneath the stars, a veil so fine,
Cloaks the remnants of a line.
Each breath a prayer, the pulse of earth,
In echoes of a newfound birth.

The past fades into soft refrain,
Yet lessons learned forever remain.
In shadows woven, soft and neat,
Are tales of strength in the wake of heat.

So linger here, in calm embrace,
As time reveals its gentle face.
For even in the darkest night,
The veils of stillness bring forth light.

Lost Songs of the Solace After Burning

From whispers lost in embers' glow,
A melody begins to flow.
In echoes soft, the heart recalls,
The songs of solace through the walls.

Where flames once danced, now silence sighs,
A haunting tune that never dies.
Each note a sigh, a tender plea,
In the breeze, the world sets free.

The ashes cradle tales untold,
Of strength and warmth that once were bold.
Yet in the stillness, hope aligns,
As lost songs weave through twisted pines.

In every heartbeat, every tear,
Lies a harmony, strong and clear.
A bittersweet reminder bright,
Of love that blooms from darkest night.

So listen close, dear wandering heart,
For solace sings in every part.
In burning flames, what fades away,
Is just a song, in bright array.

The Calm within the Charcoal Whisper

Amidst the charcoal, shadows lean,
A hidden calm, serene, unseen.
Where chaos once had carved its way,
Now rests the night, as dreams hold sway.

The gentle rustle, the softest sigh,
A whisper's touch as moments fly.
In darkened corners, secrets keep,
Woven gently as the world sleeps.

Each ember fades, yet life persists,
In every flicker, memory twists.
The calm breathes deep, it lingers still,
A promise held by nature's will.

So let the charcoal softly sing,
Of all the hope that dawn will bring.
For even in shadows, light can bloom,
A tranquil heart amidst the gloom.

In whispered tones, the spirit knows,
That from the darkest place, life grows.
Hold fast the calm, the silence be,
For in this hush, we are set free.

The Sigh of the Ashen Phoenix

In the heart of the night, a whisper starts,
A flame's gentle dance, it plays with our hearts.
From ashes, a shadow emerges anew,
Breath of the timeless, a tale tried and true.

Wings made of echoes, a song in the dark,
With every soft flutter, igniting a spark.
Through the veil of the pain, the embers arise,
A hope that will linger, beyond sorrowed skies.

In silence it rises, the phoenix prepares,
To soar through the heavens, unbinding its cares.
With each longing sigh, a promise takes flight,
A rebirth of magic, igniting the night.

Reflections in the Silenced Fire

In the chambers of dusk, a flicker slows down,
Shadows dance softly, in twilight's deep gown.
A silence unbroken, yet full of despair,
Mirrored in flames, a story laid bare.

Flickering visions in flames intertwine,
A tale forgotten, yet longing to shine.
With whispers of sorrow, and secrets to share,
The heartbeats of embers, suspended in air.

Lost in the echoes of flickering light,
Reflections weave patterns throughout the night.
What once was a blaze, now lulled to a glow,
In darkness we ponder, what we did not know.

Beneath the Weight of Lost Wings

Tattered and torn, the feathers decay,
A burden of memories, carried away.
Beneath heavy skies, a longing resides,
For the freedom of flight, where the spirit abides.

Whispers of dreams float on currents unseen,
Through shadows that dance where the memories glean.
In the silence of night, an echo remains,
Of wings once spread wide, now tethered by chains.

With every lost heartbeat, a promise still waits,
To rise from the ashes that sorrow creates.
Underneath the weight, a flicker persists,
For hope is a fire that always exists.

Melodies in the Smolder

In the hush of the morn, when the world softly sighs,
The embers still glow with a warmth that won't die.
A melody lingers, amidst ashes and dust,
Each note tells a story wrapped in wanderlust.

Through the cracks of the silence, sweet music will play,
An ode to the flames that have faded away.
With whispers of laughter that danced through the air,
In the heart of the smolder, memories still share.

In twilight's embrace, the spirits take flight,
Creating a harmony, igniting the night.
For even in endings, a song will endure,
A tale of the fire, forever pure.

Unraveled Wishes in the Fiery Mist

In the heart of the blaze, dreams take flight,
Whispers of hope through the shimmering night.
A spark in the shadows, a flicker of chance,
Unraveled wishes in a daring dance.

Embers of longing, their secrets revealed,
In the glow of the fire, our fates are sealed.
Winds carry tales of what might have been,
As flames paint the skies, where the lost dreams have
been.

Through swirling heat, the past drifts away,
Embracing the light of a brand new day.
With wishes unraveled, our spirits ignite,
In the fiery mist, we dare to take flight.

Yet, every wish born must weather the storm,
In the chaos of flames, our hearts keep warm.
For in every ember, there lies a new fate,
Unraveled desires that we cultivate.

So let the fire burn bright in your soul,
For wishes unmade can still make you whole.
In the mist of the night, let your spirit be free,
In the dance of the flames, find the essence of thee.

Celestial Reflections in Silenced Ruins

Amidst the ruins, where echoes abide,
Stars whisper softly, their secrets confide.
Reflections of ages in shadows so deep,
Celestial visions where the lost ones sleep.

Moonlit encounters with ghosts of the past,
In the stillness, their memories cast.
Winds carry stories of battles once won,
Celestial reflections, a dance with the sun.

Through broken arches, the starlight does flow,
Casting whispers of dreams from long ago.
In silence, a symphony of fate and of time,
A tapestry woven with reason and rhyme.

Here where the ancient and new intertwine,
Each stone a reminder, each shadow a sign.
Celestial reflections, they guide us anew,
In silenced ruins, we find what is true.

So take a moment, let your heart seek the light,
In the echoes of ages, let your spirit take flight.
For in every silence, a story remains,
Celestial reflections, our hopes and our pains.

The Twilight Sigh of Phoenix Echoes

In twilight's embrace, where shadows will play,
Phoenix echoes rise as the night drives away.
With wings made of fire, they soar through the dark,
A symphony woven with each whispered spark.

The sigh of the phoenix, a song of rebirth,
A promise of dawn, of renewal and worth.
In the fading light, dreams awaken anew,
As twilight whispers secrets of what we shall do.

From ashes of yore, a new chapter begins,
With courage and hope, we rise from within.
Phoenix echoes call from the depths of our soul,
In twilight's soft glow, we reclaim what is whole.

So dance in the dusk, let your spirit take wing,
For in every twilight, the phoenix will sing.
With sighs of the past, embrace what is near,
In the warmth of the twilight, our futures are clear.

As stars start to gleam, and the shadows grow long,
We stand with the echoes, united and strong.
In the heart of the twilight, with spirits aglow,
The phoenix is rising, ready to show.

Secrets in the Silence of Ash

In the stillness, beneath the gray sky,
Secrets are whispered, like dreams passing by.
The ashes lie heavy, a tale yet untold,
In silence, the echoes of courage unfold.

Each fragment a memory, a spark of the past,
Within the soft silence, the shadows are cast.
From ruins we rise, reborn from the flame,
In the silence of ash, we dare not feel shame.

For every lost story ignites hearts anew,
As whispers of hope dance in the dew.
In the quiet we gather, we stitch and we mend,
Secrets in silence, where sorrows can end.

Embrace what is hidden, and cherish the flame,
In the dark of the night, we learn not to blame.
For ashes are not just what once was consumed,
But secrets of strength that in silence are bloomed.

So listen intently, let your heart be your guide,
In the stillness of ash, let your spirit reside.
For here in the whispers, we find what is true,
Secrets in silence lead us onward anew.

Beneath the Cinders of Regret

In shadowed corners, dreams now lie,
A whisper lost, a faded sigh.
Each ember glows with tales untold,
Beneath the cinders, waning bold.

The heart remembers, though time may steal,
Fragments of joy that once felt real.
We tread the paths of what could be,
Yet find our solace beneath the tree.

Regret, a cloak that heavy drapes,
In silence, sways, as longing shapes.
But somewhere deep, a flicker stays,
To light our way through darker days.

Each crater holds a memory bright,
Yet shadows dance, a daunting sight.
And in the haze, we yearn to find,
The spark of promise, intertwined.

So breathe anew, let go, release,
For even ash can birth a fleece.
Underneath the remnants we may strive,
To listen, feel, and dream alive.

The Gentle Rumble of Hope through Smoke

Through smoky veils, a promise hums,
The gentle thrum of future drums.
Each rising wisp, a tale to share,
In whispers soft, igniting air.

Amidst despair, a lighthouse glows,
It guides the heart where courage flows.
As shadows shift and linger near,
Hope dances close, dispelling fear.

Each flicker bright, a hand to hold,
With warmth that speaks of stories bold.
And in the dark, we learn to see,
The gentle rumble, a symphony.

So let the smoke swirl round your dreams,
Find clarity in quiet streams.
For in the chaos, hope's refrain,
Will always sing through sun and rain.

Embrace the echoes, let them swell,
For even in the night, they tell.
A world awash in hairline seams,
Can weave the fabric of our dreams.

Threads of Silence in the Ashen Light

In twilight's glow, the stillness breathes,
With whispered thoughts like autumn leaves.
Each thread of silence, finely spun,
Entwines our hearts until we run.

Beneath the surface, stories ache,
With every pause, our spirits wake.
In ashen light where shadows weave,
We find the strength in all we grieve.

The world, a canvas, muted, bold,
Hides wonders deep, both new and old.
And in the gaps, the softest sighs,
Reveal the truths behind our eyes.

Yet still, the silence holds its gift,
A gentle nudge, a heart to lift.
Through quiet moments, time will strain,
And set the stage for joy and pain.

So dare to weave those threads tight-knit,
For in the quiet, we find our wit.
In ashen light, let love ignite,
And banish shadows for the night.

A Shimmer of Stillness Amongst the Blaze

In fiery storms, there lies a peace,
A shimmer soft that will not cease.
Amongst the blaze, a quiet song,
Where hearts align, we find where we belong.

With every crackle, time suspends,
And in each flicker, solace sends.
The dance of flames may twist and twine,
Yet still, we stand, our spirits shine.

In chaos spun, the calm will rise,
A glimmer seen with hopeful eyes.
And as the fire consumes the night,
We see our dreams take wing in flight.

So hold the spark that winter fends,
For every blaze, a light transcends.
In moments lost, let love embrace,
Through shifting winds, we find our place.

Amidst the heat, find tranquil ground,
A shimmer's pulse, where hope is found.
So dance within the flames that rave,
For stillness hums, even amongst the brave.

Whispers of Hope in Scorched Earth

Amidst the charred and barren land,
A heart still beats, a hopeful hand.
The winds may howl, the skies may weep,
But from the ashes, dreams will creep.

In every crack, in every stone,
A tale of courage, seeds are sown.
For even here, where shadows play,
The sun will rise, it finds a way.

The roots hold tight beneath the ground,
In silence, strength is always found.
Each droplet falls from weary skies,
Is but a whisper, not goodbyes.

Though fires rage and darkness looms,
New life will grow where silence blooms.
With every gust, a promise stirs,
A gentle hope that blurs the curs.

So take my hand, let's walk the path,
Through scorched earth's pain, we'll find the math.
With every step, the future glows,
In whispered hope, our courage grows.

The Stillness of Forgotten Flames

In corners where the shadows cling,
Forgotten flames begin to sing.
A quiet hum of what once flared,
In stillness lies the love we shared.

Around the ashes, memories twine,
Each flicker caught in lost design.
Though embers fade, they don't depart,
For still within, it warms the heart.

The air is thick with silent dreams,
Muffled whispers, soft as streams.
We linger here, though time stands still,
In warmth of night, we find our will.

Upon this ground, where silence breathes,
The echoes linger, weave, and wreathe.
In every crack, a story glows,
Of laughter shared, of love that grows.

So pause and breathe amid the night,
In darkness, find your hidden light.
For stillness speaks when flames might wane,
A quiet strength amid the pain.

Echoes of Resilience Beneath the Flames

Beneath the scorn of brilliant blaze,
Resilience hides in subtle ways.
A quiet strength, like roots in stone,
It whispers of what's yet to be known.

Amid the heat, a coolness waits,
A heartbeat strong, as fear abates.
For every scar, a badge we wear,
In tattered hopes, we find our dare.

Though flames may dance and shadows loom,
In darkest nights, we find our room.
The echoes call, with voices clear,
That rise above the throes of fear.

In swirling fire, we stand our ground,
With hands held tight, our strength is found.
For in the blaze, the spirit run,
We forge ahead, the battle's won.

So let the flames burn bright and high,
With every flicker, we learn to fly.
Through ashes soft, through trials vast,
The echoes of strength remain steadfast.

The Lament of Ash and Dusk

When silence falls on ash-strewn ground,
A lament rises, yet so profound.
In dusky light, the shadows blend,
To weave a tale that time can't end.

For every ember that flickers low,
A story whispers, soft and slow.
In grief, there lies a fragile thread,
Of love and life, forever wed.

The twilight hums a mournful tune,
A melody beneath the moon.
For though the fire has since died,
In every heart, memories bide.

The air grows thick with unspoken words,
A symphony of flightless birds.
In shadows cast, the dreams rewind,
To touch the lost, to seek the blind.

So gather close, as dusk prevails,
In softest whispers, hope unveils.
For ash and dusk, in stillness blend,
A love unbroken, without end.

Traces of Light in the Ember's Grasp

In the glow of twilight's dim embrace,
A tender warmth finds its rightful place.
Whispers of dreams through the shadows play,
While the embers dance at the close of day.

Beneath the stars, in a velvet night,
Flickers of hope awaken from plight.
Each spark a promise, a story untold,
In the heart of the fire, brave spirits bold.

Through deepened paths where the shadows creep,
Echoes of laughter in silence seep.
Threads of connection like tendrils entwined,
In the ember's grasp, true magic defined.

With every flicker, a memory sways,
Of battles forged in both darkness and rays.
The light we nurture, though fleeting at best,
Is a beacon of solace, a burning quest.

So let us gather 'round warmth of the fire,
In the ember's glow, our spirits aspire.
Together we rise, in the shadows we stand,
Tracing the light, hand in trembling hand.

Synchronized Silence Within Smoldering Shadows

In the stillness where twilight takes flight,
A hush envelops the encroaching night.
Smoldering shadows breathe soft and slow,
Holding the secrets that silence bestows.

Whispers of twilight, a mystical dance,
In synchronized silence, we find our chance.
With hearts entwined in the shroud of the dark,
Each flicker of warmth igniting a spark.

Ghosts of the past in the shadows we trace,
Finding the light in a sacred space.
Through the calm of the stillness, we feel the thread,
Connecting our souls to the words left unsaid.

Glimmers of fire cast dreams in the breeze,
As rapture awakens with effortless ease.
Under a canopy of shimmering night,
We dance with the echoes, embracing our light.

And in this twilight, through shadows we see,
Each moment unravels, forever to be.
Synchronized rhythms, eternal we find,
In the smoldering silence, our hearts intertwined.

Flickering Memories in Ashen Elysium

In ashen expanse where the embers decay,
Flickering memories begin to sway.
Haunted by echoes of laughter and cheer,
The warmth of the past draws painfully near.

Beneath the layers of soot and of time,
A whisper of hope, a fragile rhyme.
Lost in the shadows, we seek out the light,
To reclaim our joy in the depths of the night.

Winds carry tales of forgotten delight,
As shadows reach out, obscuring our sight.
Yet through the darkness, we brave the unknown,
In ashen Elysium, seeds of light sown.

Through flickering flames, our hearts begin to mend,
Tracing the paths where the memories blend.
Each scar an emblem of battles survived,
In the glare of the embers, our spirits revived.

So let us remember the flickers we've lost,
In the ashen embrace, love knows not the cost.
For even in sorrow, there's beauty sold,
In the winding journey, our stories unfold.

Introspection in the Wake of Firestorms

In the aftermath, where silence prevails,
Beneath the wreckage of smoldering trails.
We delve inwards, our hearts laid bare,
Finding our strength in the ashes we share.

Reflections shimmer like dew on the grass,
In the wake of the firestorms, moments pass.
Each flicker a lesson, a truth to behold,
In the chaos of life, our spirits unfold.

With every shadow that threatens to bind,
The light of resilience, we seek and we find.
Through fire and fury, we weather the storm,
In the depths of our trials, our courage is born.

And when the tempest begins to recede,
With hearts open wide, we honor the seeds.
For in the reflection of what we have faced,
Hope springs eternal, destruction effaced.

In introspection, we gather the threads,
Woven through struggles, the path that we've tread.
Emerging united, our spirits ignite,
In the wake of the firestorms, we reclaim our light.

Shadows Linger in the Fiery Twilight

In twilight's glow, the shadows play,
Whispers of night begin to sway.
Stars ignite in the ink-black sea,
While dreams unfold, wild and free.

The trees stand guard, a silent brigade,
Casting long tales in the dying shade.
As colors bleed in the evening sky,
Memories linger, a soft goodbye.

The fire crackles with playful glee,
Sparks dancing like spirit-set free.
In the dusk's embrace, secrets confide,
Painting the night with dreams beside.

Each flicker tells a story untold,
Of brave hearts and treasures of gold.
In the dusk, as the world seems to sigh,
Hope is reborn in the twilight sky.

With the fading light, our hearts take flight,
Chasing the echoes of the night.
In shadows deep, where mysteries bloom,
We find our path in the softening gloom.

Sooty Reveries of the Lost Dream

In the depths of night, whispers breathe,
Sooty dreams on the edge of seethe.
Lost in the twilight's gentle embrace,
Forgotten wishes, a faded trace.

The fireplace crackles, memories flare,
Dust motes swirling, magic in the air.
Ghosts of laughter, we once held dear,
Drift like echoes, both far and near.

Through the window, shadows creep,
Carrying secrets that time will keep.
Veils of the past flutter soft and light,
In the stillness, they dance through the night.

With every breath, old tales revive,
In the solitude, the lost dreams thrive.
Yet visions fade as dawn breaks near,
Leaving behind just a whispering tear.

In sooty reveries, our hearts do roam,
Searching the corridors of lost home.
For in the night, when the world rests still,
Dreams awaken, and our hearts they fill.

Beneath the Armour of Ember Grey

Beneath the skies, of ember grey,
The past and present twist and sway.
Guarded by shadows, we walk alone,
In a world where the wild has grown.

Whispers linger in the smoky air,
Stories of courage, of love laid bare.
Each step we take on this ancient ground,
Hearts entwined, in silence profound.

The branches cradle, the secrets they keep,
Memories woven in the fabric of sleep.
Under the twilight, so soft and deep,
A promise lingers, a bond to reap.

In the hearth's glow, our spirits ignite,
Fires of dreams burst forth from the night.
With every ember that flickers and sways,
We forge our hopes in the twilight's haze.

For beneath the stillness, the ember's glow,
Lies the strength that we seldom show.
And as the shadows dance their play,
Our hearts stay strong in the ember grey.

The Dance of Silence in the Burning Woods

In burning woods, where silence breathes,
The dance of shadows weaves through leaves.
With every step, the whispers rise,
Echoing softly 'neath silvered skies.

Fires flicker, paint the trees,
Glimmers of magic in warm, soft breeze.
The earth awakes with a gentle sigh,
As stars peak out from the darkening sky.

Moonlight spills like a silken thread,
Guiding the lost, where dreams have fled.
Each flickering flame reveals the lost,
In the burning woods, we dance, no cost.

With every twirl, the night unfolds,
Stories of old, through the forest told.
In dance and silence, we come alive,
For in the stillness, our spirits thrive.

Through the burning woods, our hearts will soar,
In the dance of silence, forevermore.
With hands held tight in the shadows' embrace,
We find our home in this sacred place.

Muted Echoes from the Heart of the Flames

In the silence where embers sigh,
Whispers dance beneath the sky.
Memories flicker, soft and bright,
Bound in shadows, lost to night.

Fragments of laughter, bittersweet,
Echoing as they softly meet.
Each heartbeat sings a tale untold,
In the warmth, the truth unfolds.

The flames consume, yet do they save?
Crafting stories, brave and grave.
In charred remains, the soul's refrain,
Burns eternal in joy and pain.

Through ashes bright, the past does blend,
In fiery courses, paths extend.
Ghostly figures, they take their stance,
In the flickering glow, they twirl, they dance.

Fading light, a gentle plea,
From the flames, we seek to be.
Unified in the ember's hum,
From these echoes, we shall come.

Flickering Hope in the Dusty Gloom

In corners worn by time's embrace,
A glimmer shines in shadowed space.
Hope hangs like dust in the air,
A promise whispered, soft and rare.

Through weary hours, we must believe,
In dreams unspoken, we find reprieve.
Each flicker snares the night's deep sigh,
A tender wish that dares to fly.

Beyond the darkness, a beacon glows,
Guiding hearts where the river flows.
In the silence, we gather near,
To hold the light, to face our fear.

With every shadow that dares to creep,
We plant the seeds where promise sleeps.
In dusty corners, hope shall bloom,
Defying ever the weight of gloom.

Through trials fierce, we share our dreams,
In unity, we weave our seams.
A flickering dance, our hands entwined,
Hope in the dusk, forever aligned.

The Soft Embrace of a New Dawn

In the hush before the light appears,
A gentle touch dispels our fears.
Morning whispers, bright and clear,
Inviting souls to draw near.

A canvas spreads, hues interlace,
Painting dreams with tender grace.
Sunrise dances on the hill,
Chasing shadows, moments still.

Each ray a promise, fresh and bright,
Guiding lost hearts to take flight.
In every dewdrop, hope is found,
In the silence, blessings abound.

Through the cracks where darkness clings,
New beginnings softly sing.
A symphony of light reborn,
In the embrace of the early morn.

We gather strength from dawn's sweet song,
With brave hearts, we know we belong.
In warmth of light, our spirits soar,
Together steadfast, forevermore.

Shadows Cradle the Flickers of Tomorrow

In twilight's clasp, where dreams descend,
Shadows cradle what we defend.
Flickers of hope weave through the night,
Crafting visions, bold and bright.

Threads of silver in the dark,
Each spark ignites an ancient arc.
In the stillness, whispers rise,
Reflecting truths in the starlit skies.

Through paths unknown, we dare to tread,
On flickering lights, our hearts are fed.
Tomorrow's echoes softly call,
In dance of shadows, we rise or fall.

Embers of courage refuse to fade,
In the darkest night, they're unafraid.
Grasping dreams with tender might,
We seek the dawn, embrace the light.

So let us wander where shadows play,
With flickers guiding our way.
Together we'll write this tale anew,
Where shadows cradle dreams that grew.

Serenity at the Edge of the Inferno

In shadows where the embers glow,
Peace whispers softly, warm and slow.
A flicker dances, then takes flight,
As starlight guides through endless night.

Fires may roar, their hunger vast,
Yet in the stillness, strength is cast.
The heart remembers, fierce and true,
A tranquil spirit, born anew.

Beneath the flames, a heartbeat thrum,
A promise made to rise, not succumb.
With every pulse, a soothing breath,
Serenity blooms, defying death.

From ashes rise the dreams once lost,
Echoing whispers of love's soft frost.
The edge of darkness holds the light,
In the inferno, hope ignites.

Evermore, the dance persists,
In twilight's grip, the chaos twists.
Clarity flows like a gentle stream,
Serenity thrives where shadows dream.

Gentle Strokes Over the Searing Darkness

Beneath the cloak of fiery hue,
A gentle touch breaks through anew.
With every brush, the heart takes flight,
Over the darkness, strokes of light.

Each spark a story, brave and bold,
Woven tales of dreams retold.
In silence, peace begins to spread,
Over the chaos where fear once tread.

The darkness quivers, spirits sigh,
Yearning for dawn to claim the sky.
Tenderness weaves through pain and ache,
In gentle strokes, the world will wake.

Painting hope with colors bright,
A canvas born of endless night.
Brush aside the smoky veil,
And watch the whispers start to sail.

Through every stroke, the promise gleams,
Awakening the lostest dreams.
From searing depths, we rise and grow,
With gentle strokes, the light will flow.

Echoing Spirits in the Scorched Sky

Beneath the vast and burning dome,
Whispers of spirits call us home.
In echoes threaded through the flames,
Their stories linger, soft refrains.

From cinders rise the tales of old,
Of battles fought and glories bold.
In the ashes, dreams still gleam,
Echoing softly, like a dream.

Voices weave through twilight's shroud,
In every cry, the shadows bowed.
Spirits dance in fiery embrace,
Guiding hearts through empty space.

As stars align in scarlet plight,
They remind us of hope's pure light.
In the scorched sky, their laughter thrives,
A melody that never dies.

Beyond the flames, we hear their song,
A harmony where we belong.
Through echoing spirits, we reclaim,
The dreamers' path, the eternal flame.

The Calm Before the Resurgence

In twilight's hush, we hold our breath,
A lingering pause before the depth.
The stillness whispers, soft and sweet,
A gentle promise where hopes meet.

The air electric, charged with fate,
As worlds align in silence wait.
Stars shimmer softly, tucked away,
Before the dawn that leads to day.

Moments stretch into a sigh,
In the calm, the spirits fly.
A lullaby, pure and divine,
Spinning tales of the grand design.

Yet shadows linger, poised to leap,
In this sweet calm, the secrets keep.
Rising tides of change unwind,
A surge of hope for hearts aligned.

Beneath the surface, flames ignite,
The promise swells, ready for flight.
In the calm before the great rise,
Awakens life beneath the skies.

Gossamer Dreams in the Charcoal Night

In the stillness, shadows weave,
Whispers of dreams we dare believe.
Moonlight glimmers on hidden streams,
As we sail on gossamer dreams.

Darkness cradles the whispered lore,
Secrets lie behind each closed door.
Starlit secrets invite our flight,
To chase the beauty of the night.

Laced with magic, the night unfolds,
Stories of wonder, soft and bold.
With each heartbeat, the cosmos sighs,
Eternal hopes dance in our eyes.

Through the veils of twilight's embrace,
We find our hearts in this sacred space.
Colors shimmer in emerald light,
As we wander the world of night.

And in this realm where wishes gleam,
We find our path, a shimmering beam.
With every breath, freedom ignites,
In gossamer dreams, we take flight.

Rebirth From the Quiet Depths

From depths unseen, new life shall rise,
Awakening under the tranquil skies.
Silence stirs, the unseen breaks,
In whispered breaths, the stillness wakes.

Gentle ripples on a crystal brook,
Each soft murmur, a hopeful look.
Through shadows deep, we weave our thread,
In quiet growth, new paths are led.

Emerging softly, the dawn appears,
Washing away the weight of years.
With each heartbeat, the future sways,
Rebirth beckons in tender ways.

The roots reach deep, yet skies adore,
In every bud, the promise to explore.
Life unfolds in hues so bright,
A symphony born from the night.

In the garden where quiet calls,
Resilience blooms, as beauty sprawls.
From stillness springs a vibrant breath,
A dance of life, rebirth from death.

Composure Amidst the Fiery Chaos

In tempest's heart, where shadows clash,
A single breath becomes a flash.
Through flames that roar and embers that fly,
We find our peace, let worries die.

With steady hands and calm within,
The chaos sings, yet we begin.
In swirling reds and vibrant yellows,
Our hearts unite, steadfast and mellow.

Each flicker tells of strength untold,
A dance of passion, fierce and bold.
Amidst the storm, we heed the call,
In fiery chaos, we stand tall.

With eyes alight, we chart our course,
Navigating with an inner force.
In the furnace, we forge our dreams,
Transforming fear into vibrant themes.

Through chaos fierce, the calm we hold,
In flames of life, our courage unfolds.
Embracing chaos, we find our way,
Composure leads us, come what may.

Stillness Where the Sparks Dance

In twilight's hush, a moment's grace,
Stillness found in a sacred place.
Where sparks alight, and shadows twirl,
In gentle rhythms, dreams unfurl.

A quiet heart in a fevered world,
Amidst the flames, a flag unfurled.
The air ignites with whispered chance,
In this stillness, the sparks dance.

With every flicker, secrets weave,
A tapestry for those who believe.
In silence, possibilities glance,
Casting spells in a luminous trance.

We gather close, where the fire flares,
In joy and wonder, we shed our cares.
Bathed in warmth, we feel the trance,
In this stillness, the sparks dance.

Whispers of magic drawn from the night,
Through the sparks, we find our light.
In each heartbeat, a song of chance,
A timeless waltz, where the sparks dance.

Pause Amidst the Fire's Lament

In embers' glow, the shadows dance,
A fleeting glimpse, a whispered chance.
The flames that crackle, hearts eclipse,
Amidst the smoke, the spirit slips.

Yet in the chaos, courage stands,
Braving the blaze with open hands.
With every spark, a truth is born,
In ash and ruin, hope is sworn.

For every tear that quenches fire,
Springs forth a wish, a fierce desire.
To rise anew, from chaos spun,
A tale of light, when day is done.

So let the heart not fear to weep,
In loss, there lies the promise deep.
For even flames, though fierce and bright,
Yield to the dawn, and fade from sight.

In moments still, amidst the fight,
We gather courage, summon light.
A phoenix waits within the ash,
Ready to soar, and break the brash.

A Gentle Breath Above the Scorched Earth

Above the land where sorrow sleeps,
A breath of wind, the silence weeps.
Each grain of sand, a whispered prayer,
For solace found in open air.

With fragile wings, the spirits soar,
A melody from yonder shore.
The scars that mar this earthly plane,
Shall bloom anew from sorrow's rain.

In twilight's hush, the stars will gleam,
A haven formed from shattered dream.
For even in the darkest night,
The gentle breath shall usher light.

With every sigh that stirs the trees,
Comes forth the promise of sweet ease.
A dance of shadows, soft and bright,
Transforms the earth, restores the light.

Beneath the clouds that veil the sun,
The battle lost, yet hope not done.
Each heartbeat thrums with life anew,
In gentle breath, the world breaks through.

Beneath the Weight of Ashes

Beneath the ashes, stories lie,
Dreams once bold, now sighing high.
In silent depths where shadows blend,
The whispered echoes never end.

Yet from the char, a pulse remains,
Hidden beneath the hurtful stains.
Hope flickers faint, a stubborn fire,
In every heart, a buried choir.

With gentle hands, we lift the veil,
Unearth the truth where spirits wail.
For life persists in sacred ground,
In every heartbeat, love is found.

Embers speak of time long lost,
But life will rise despite the cost.
A journey fraught with pain and grace,
We find our strength, reclaim our space.

So let the ashes guide the way,
To brighter dawns and fairer days.
For from the weight, we learn to soar,
With hearts alight and spirits roar.

Tension Thaws

In stillness, there a tension brews,
A fragile line, the heart must choose.
Between the known and paths unknown,
The seeds of fate have deeply grown.

As icy glares give way to dawn,
The heavy heart begins to yawn.
A breath releases, soft and sweet,
To clear the air, make harmony meet.

Each moment stretched, yet time will bend,
As warmth creeps in, the soul can mend.
The weight of doubt begins to fade,
In love's embrace, new life is made.

With every smile, the silence breaks,
And tension weaves in gentle wakes.
For in the thaw, our spirits sing,
Of joys to come, and hope in spring.

So may the heart, once locked in fear,
Find strength in trust, and draw you near.
To where the sun caresses skies,
And love's sweet warmth forever flies.

The Unseen Tides of Rebirth

The moonlit waves caress the shore,
A dance of tides, forevermore.
In silence deep, the waters churn,
And from the dark, new worlds we learn.

Each ebb and flow, a tale unfolds,
Of brave new lives, and dreams untold.
For in the depths, both light and shade,
Awaits the spark where hope is made.

Beneath the surface, life abides,
In currents strong, the spirit slides.
An unseen force, both vast and wise,
Brings forth the dawn, where spirit flies.

In every heartbeat, rhythms play,
The tides of change, they shape the day.
With every breath, we find our worth,
In unseen tides, we are rebirth.

So ride the waves, let courage steer,
Embrace the flow, let go of fear.
For in the dance, we find our place,
The unseen tides, of love's embrace.

Faint Heartbeats of a Fallen Hero

In shadows deep where whispers dwell,
A hero's heart, now hushed, can tell.
Of battles fought with courage vast,
Yet in the quiet, echoes cast.

The brave can fall, the brave can fade,
But in the still, their dreams are laid.
Each heartbeat strong, though silent now,
Still wings in time, they shall not bow.

A memory drapes the evening sky,
With starlit tears that never die.
In every heart that dares to soar,
A glimpse of grace lost evermore.

With mournful hymns the night can sing,
For tales of love and loss they bring.
Yet hope persists, like morning dew,
For heroes' fires will pierce the blue.

So raise a glass, let voices blend,
To those who fought and dared to bend.
In every heart, their courage dwells,
A faint heartbeat, their story tells.

Pensive Moments in the Wake of the Flame

Beneath the ash where shadows grow,
A silent flame once danced, aglow.
Now flickers dim in twilight's grasp,
A whisper slow, an ember's clasp.

The wind it weaves a tale of night,
Of fleeting joy and lost delight.
In pensive thoughts, we seek the past,
Where warmth once dwelled, now shadows cast.

The echoes of the fire's song,
Once fiercely bright, now faint and long.
Each moment shared, a treasure lost,
In memories held, we bear the cost.

Yet still we hope, though hearts may ache,
In every spark, new dreams we make.
For in the dark, a light we find,
Rekindling faith, with love entwined.

So let us gather, hearts aflame,
To honor those who bore the name.
In pensive moments, deep and true,
We'll share the warmth, with love anew.

Threads of Smoke and Silent Grace

In twilight's weave, the shadows lie,
A dance of smoke, as whispers fly.
Each thread a story, soft and bold,
Of silent grace and dreams retold.

The stars they beckon, twinkle near,
While hopes ascend, despite the fear.
With silver threads, we stitch the night,
In patterns woven with pure light.

The nightingale's lament draws near,
As echoes fade, yet still we hear.
In silent grace, in moments bare,
We find the strength that lingers there.

For in the smoke, a truth we see,
Of love that binds, of what can be.
Each heartbeat thrums in quiet space,
A tapestry of time and grace.

So let us dance, in shadows bright,
With threads of hope, we'll weave the light.
In smoke's embrace, our spirits rise,
To greet the dawn, where promise lies.

Ashfall upon Unbroken Wings

Upon the ground, the ashes lay,
A tale of flight, now lost in gray.
Yet in the still, a rustle stirs,
Of dreams that soar, undimmed by blur.

The phoenix rises from the dust,
With wings of flame, and vibrant trust.
For every fall, a chance to grow,
In ashes deep, the embers glow.

A whispering breeze through valleys wide,
Calls forth the heart, with joy and pride.
Unbroken wings, they brush the skies,
In every tear, a truth that flies.

Though shadows fall, and darkness reign,
The spirit dances, free from pain.
In every heart, the fire sings,
Of hope reborn on radiant wings.

So let the ashes mark the ground,
For life renews, where love is found.
In each ascent, a story starts,
Unbroken wings, and tender hearts.

Beneath the Smoke

In shadows where the whispers dwell,
A tale of magic weaves its spell.
The air is thick, the heart beats fast,
Beneath the smoke, our die is cast.

Ghostly figures dance in light,
Flickering, fading, out of sight.
Each secret held within the night,
A promise stolen from our flight.

A hidden path through twisted trees,
Where laughter mingles with the breeze.
The embers glow with ancient lore,
Awakening dreams we can't ignore.

Yet shadows loom, intentions veiled,
With every breath, our silence hailed.
A lingering doubt weighs on our hearts,
As certainty from hope departs.

Together we face the chilling dark,
Embracing fear, igniting spark.
For beneath the smoke, we find our way,
A flicker of hope, come what may.

Seeds of Tomorrow

In gardens where the silence grows,
A whisper from the earth bestows.
Each seed a wish, a dream to sow,
In soil of time, the future flows.

With every rain that softly falls,
A melody of nature calls.
The roots entwine beneath our feet,
In harmony our hearts do beat.

The sun will rise, the shadows fade,
In warmth and light, our plans are laid.
The promise of a bright tomorrow,
Dispersing all our past's deep sorrow.

Hope's gentle touch in every sprout,
The faith we hold, the dreams we sprout.
With every dawn, new stories bloom,
In vibrant hues, dispelling gloom.

So plant your dreams, let courage soar,
In fields of gold, you'll find much more.
For seeds of tomorrow, rich and bold,
Are worth their weight in stories told.

Whispers in the Ashen Dawn

As night retreats, the embers spark,
A canvas drawn, both bright and dark.
Whispers mingle with the cool air,
In the dawn's embrace, dreams lay bare.

The ashes dance, a fleeting grace,
With secrets of a forgotten place.
Each flicker tells a tale of yore,
Sparks of magic to explore.

Through misty veils of fading light,
New chances beckon, pure and bright.
With every breath, our hopes entwine,
In the silence, a world divine.

The morning breaks, a soft refrain,
As nature sings through joy and pain.
For in the ashes, life must rise,
With every dawn, a new surprise.

So gather 'round, as shadows flee,
And let the day set your spirit free.
For whispers linger, soft and true,
In the ashen dawn, they'll guide you through.

Echoes of a Fading Flame

In twilight's grip, where echoes dwell,
The stories forged, a magic spell.
With every flicker, voices call,
The fading flame, a dance, a fall.

What once burned bright now dims with time,
But still within, a subtle rhyme.
A heartbeat shared, a fleeting trace,
In memories held, we find our place.

The ember's glow, a sacred trust,
As shadows weave through dreams of dust.
A tether strong, though time may wane,
Within our hearts, the fire's reign.

So gather 'round this fragile light,
Let warmth embrace you through the night.
For though the flame may fade away,
The echoes linger and softly stay.

In whispered thoughts and tender sighs,
The essence lives, it never dies.
With echoes of a fading flame,
We'll hold on tight, forever claim.

Solitude Beneath the Ember Sky

Beneath the vast and starry dome,
In solitude, we find our home.
The embers glow, a gentle guide,
Through quiet nights, where dreams abide.

In the stillness, thoughts take flight,
Like fireflies in the velvet night.
Each breath a vow, each pulse a song,
In solitude, we can belong.

With every flicker dances hope,
A fragile thread, a way to cope.
In the whispers, truth appears,
As laughter mingles with the tears.

The sky ablaze with ancient lore,
Inviting us to seek for more.
In solitude beneath this hue,
We find the strength to start anew.

So let the stars be our embrace,
In this vast and sacred space.
Together, though perhaps alone,
We make this world our very own.

Soft Strokes of Renewal Among the Ruins

In shadows deep where whispers play,
Soft tendrils rise from earth's decay.
Forgotten seeds, in silence sown,
Awake to life, as hope is grown.

Beneath the stone, a single flower,
Emerges bold, reclaiming power.
With petals bright, it greets the dawn,
A tender heart where faith is drawn.

Through twilight's veil, the sun retreats,
While new beginnings softly greet.
Among the ruins, life will thrive,
To weave the past, and thus survive.

So listen close, to nature's song,
In every creak where roots belong.
The softest strokes can mend the pain,
And from the loss, the blooms remain.

Delicate Threads in a World of Ember

In the glow of fading light,
Threads of silver take their flight.
Woven dreams in twilight's grace,
Dance like fireflies in this space.

Among the ashes, hope is spun,
A tapestry of life begun.
Each fragile strand, a story told,
Revealing warmth in bitter cold.

With gentle hands, we stitch anew,
A bond of hearts, a steadfast crew.
In embers' glow, our spirits rise,
Together soaring toward the skies.

The silence speaks, a whispered prayer,
For every soul that lingers there.
Delicate threads that intertwine,
In a world of loss, we still shine.

Gentle Reflections in a Fading Fire

Upon the hearth, the embers glow,
Their flickered light begins to slow.
In gentle whispers, dreams ascend,
As memories of the night's descend.

Each flame a laugh, each spark a tear,
Soft reflections of those held dear.
With every shadow cast so sly,
Old stories linger, never die.

The fire's warmth, a tender balm,
In quiet moments, steady, calm.
We gather close, with hearts in tow,
Around the hushed, resplendent glow.

In fading light, our hopes take flight,
As stars appear, a jeweled sight.
So hold them close, these fleeting hours,
For in the night, our spirit flowers.

Subtle Signs of Life on the Charred Horizon

On charred horizons, stillness reigns,
Yet life stirs softly through the grains.
A broken branch that bends anew,
A testament of what is true.

In silence wrapped, the earth can heal,
With gentle force, the heart will feel.
Among the ruins, hope extends,
In quiet grace, the struggle ends.

The sun dips low, a golden hue,
As shadows stretch to welcome you.
Subtle signs in every crevice,
A promise held, a soft premise.

Life finds a way, though battles scar,
With every moment, we raise the bar.
In ashes deep, resilience shines,
On charred horizons, fate aligns.

Dreamscapes in the Heart of Fire

In twilight's gaze, the embers dance,
Whispers of secrets, a fleeting chance.
Through fiery realms, courage ignites,
Where shadows twirl, and hope alights.

Beneath the blaze, old fears dissolve,
A heart remembers, a soul evolves.
With every spark, dreams take their flight,
In the heart of fire, we find our light.

Time drips slowly, like molten gold,
Every story, fervently told.
In crimson tales, we face the pyre,
Crafting worlds from the heart of fire.

Embers like kisses on softest skin,
Feelings awaken, they beckon within.
In this realm where darkness bows,
We forge our futures, ignite our vows.

So dance with flames, let worries flee,
In this vast space, we are truly free.
For in the blaze, our spirits soar,
Dreamscapes thrive on forevermore.

Fluttering Hearts Amidst Rebirth

Amidst the ash, new life begins,
Like fragile fluttering that softly spins.
From sorrow's depth, a melody's rise,
Hearts learn to dream beneath open skies.

In gentle springs where hope is sown,
Resilient blooms, by love overgrown.
Each petal whispers of courage true,
In the joyous light, we find what's due.

Winds of change lift spirits high,
While clouds disperse in the cerulean sky.
The warmth of laughter breaks through the chill,
Rebirth is a promise, profound and still.

Together we weave through trials endured,
With threads of kindness, our souls assured.
Fluttering hearts in this grand ballet,
Dance through the twilight, come what may.

So hold on tight, to dreams ignited,
In the face of shadows, we're united.
For amidst rebirth, we learn to soar,
Fluttering hearts, forevermore.

Fragments of Sound in the Ember Drift

Upon the breeze, whispers take flight,
Fragments of sound in the soft twilight.
Each echo dances amid the smoke,
Songs of the brave, softly they invoke.

Through the forest, where shadows blend,
Melodies linger, as daylight bends.
Every note tells of battles won,
In the ember drift, new journeys begun.

Chimes of laughter pierce through the haze,
A symphony born from forgotten days.
With each heartbeat, the rhythm calls,
In the soft embrace, destiny sprawls.

So listen close, let the whispers steer,
In the depths of night, let go of fear.
For in the quiet, the loudest truths thrive,
Fragments of sound help us survive.

In this melody, life's essence flows,
Through darkened paths, a calmness bestows.
In ember drift, the heart learns to mend,
Harmony blossoms, on love we depend.

The Softest Glow in the Charred Abyss

In the depths of night, shadows reside,
Yet hope brings warmth, like a gentle guide.
Through charred remains, a glow appears,
The softest light drowns out our fears.

With every flicker, a story unfolds,
Reminders of dreams that the heart still holds.
In the darkest corners, strength is found,
A whisper of love in the silent ground.

As stars shimmer through the ink-black skies,
We find our courage, we learn to rise.
In the charred abyss, we gather our might,
Crafting from ashes, our path ignites.

So hold onto flames, let them be known,
For even in deep, we're never alone.
The softest glow will lead the way,
Through the charred abyss to a brand new day.

In every shadow, a promise lies,
A flicker of hope that never dies.
From the depths of night, we carve our bliss,
With the softest glow, in the charred abyss.

The Silence of Growth in Burnt Remnants

In ashes deep, the seeds take root,
Amidst the black, a whispered fruit.
From charred remains, a dream will sprout,
In silence fierce, there lies a route.

Beneath the soil, the tendrils creep,
Awakening hope from restful sleep.
Each droplet blessed, a soothing balm,
In quiet strength, the world feels calm.

Forgotten stones, they hold the past,
Yet life renews, its shadow cast.
From fire's edge, a vibrant hue,
As whispers chant the life anew.

The wind, a muse, it carries soft,
While dreams reborn, they soar aloft.
In beauty forged from what has burned,
The silence speaks of all we've learned.

With patience draped in evening's veil,
The tale unfolds, a gentle trail.
In burnt remnants, the future sings,
And from the ashes, growth takes wings.

Hidden Colors of a Silent Resurgence

In muted shades where shadows dwell,
The heart of night casts out its spell.
Among the hues of twilight's sigh,
The hidden colors start to fly.

As nightingale sings softly here,
Awakens life, dispels the fear.
With whispers wrapped in velvet skies,
The world reveals its sweet surprise.

Each petal wakes from silver dreams,
A tapestry of muted schemes.
In silent dance, the colors blend,
To greet the dawn as night must end.

With every glimmer, hope ignites,
Within the quiet, hidden lights.
A resurgent pulse, so tender, bright,
Restores the soul and warms the night.

And in the hush, we learn to see,
The beauty cradled quietly.
For in the dark, the colors play,
As life unfolds in soft ballet.

Hushed Harmony Among the Cinders

From cinders cold, a symphony,
In quietude, there's clarity.
Each ember hums a soft refrain,
Of memories forged through joy and pain.

The world begins to breathe anew,
As harmony between the blue.
In twilight's hush, the echoes call,
A melody that binds us all.

With whispered chords and gentle strife,
The past, it weaves the threads of life.
Among the cinders, beauty's found,
In whispered notes that swirl around.

Through shadows cast by fleeting light,
The heart finds dance in the night.
In every sigh, a promise sways,
As hushed harmonies weave days.

In cinder's glow, we come alive,
With every note, our spirits thrive.
Together in this quiet song,
Among the remnants, we belong.

The Serene Dance of Becoming

In shadows deep, the dance begins,
A serenade to fragile sins.
With every step, the world conspires,
To lift our souls and spark desires.

The rhythm flows, a gentle tide,
With grace, we learn to bide and ride.
In softest light, we shed the old,
And in our hearts, new dreams unfold.

With whispered vows, the stars align,
A tapestry of fate divine.
In every swirl, the past is known,
As we embrace the seeds we've sown.

In stillness found, we learn to dance,
A waltz of hope, a sweet romance.
For every wound that time bestows,
In tranquil steps, resilience grows.

The moonlight bathes us in its glow,
As winds of change begin to blow.
With open arms, we greet the dawn,
In serene dance, our fears are gone.

www.ingramcontent.com/pod-product-compliance
Ingram Content Group UK Ltd.
Pitfield, Milton Keynes, MK11 3LW, UK
UKHW021503280125
4335UKWH00035B/681